Donovan McNabb

Donovan McNabb

Michael Bradley

BENCHMARK BOOKS

MARSHALL CAVENDISH
NEW YORK

Benchmark Books
Marshall Cavendish
99 White Plains Road
Tarrytown, NY 10591-9001
www.marshallcavendish.com

Library of Congress Cataloging-in-Publication Data

Bradley, Michael, 1962–
Donovan McNabb / by Michael Bradley.
p. cm.—(Benchmark all-stars)
Includes bibliographical references (p.   ) and index.
Contents: Back to greatness—Laying the foundation—College days—
The big time—On the verge—The promised land—almost—
Player statistics.
ISBN 0-7614-1756-7
1. McNabb, Donovan—Juvenile literature. 2. Football players—United
States—Biography—Juvenile literature. [1. McNabb, Donovan. 2. Football
players. 3. African Americans—Biography.] I. Title II. Series:
Bradley, Michael, 1962– , Benchmark all-stars.

GV939.M38B73 2004
796.332'092—dc22

2003026075

Photo Research by Regina Flanagan
Cover photograph: AP/Wide World Photos
Greg Fiume/NewSport/Corbis: 2–3; Steve Boyle/NewSport/Corbis: 6;
AP/Wide World Photos: 8, 9, 10, 11, 14, 17, 18, 20, 22, 29, 31, 41, 42;
Al Tielemans/Sports Illustrated: 12; Bob Rosato/Sports Illustrated : 23;
STR/Reuters: 26; AFP/Corbis: 31,32,40; Anthony Bolante/Reuters: 35;
Reuters NewMedia/Corbis: 36; Sue Ogrocki/Reuters: 37; Tim Shaffer/Reuters: 38; Drew
Hollowell/Icon Sports Media: 44.

Series design by Becky Terhune
Printed in Italy
1 3 5 6 4 2

Contents

Chapter One | Back to Greatness 7

Chapter Two | Laying the Foundation 13

Chapter Three | College Days 21

Chapter Four | The Big Time 27

Chapter Five | On the Verge 33

Chapter Six | The Promised Land—Almost 39

Player Statistics 44

Glossary 46

Find Out More 47

Index 48

Philadelphia Eagles Donovan
McNabb throws another winning pass!

CHAPTER ONE

Back to Greatness

*T*here were questions. Big ones. After missing six weeks of the 2002 National Football League (NFL) season with a broken ankle, Donovan McNabb was back in the lineup and under center for the Philadelphia Eagles. It was playoff time, and McNabb was ready. Ready to lead. Ready to star. Ready to prove that he could play.

Many wondered whether McNabb could do it. He had missed too much time and did not prepare enough for the Eagles' opponent, the Atlanta Falcons. He would be rusty, slow, and afraid of contact. Some Philadelphia fans thought that coach Andy Reid should stay with A. J. Feeley, the third-stringer who had led the Eagles to a 4-1 record while McNabb was out. His leg may have healed, but McNabb would not be able to run as well as he had before. He could not take a big hit. He wouldn't be, well, McNabb.

"According to everyone else, I'm not mobile, or I'm not able to move anymore," McNabb said. "I'll just let people continue to think that. When the time comes, we'll showcase that a little."

The time came almost right away. On the Eagles' second play from scrimmage, McNabb was chased out of the pocket by Falcons defenders. He headed for the right sideline, and instead of sneaking out of bounds, he turned upfield and dashed for 19 yards. Questions answered. McNabb was just fine.

During a game against the Cardinals, McNabb injured his right ankle so badly he spent the rest of the season on the bench.

"That was the run I was waiting to see," then-Eagles wide receiver Antonio Freeman said after the game. "When I saw that, I said, 'He's back,' and I'm sure everybody else did, too."

McNabb had answered the questions about his health with the run. He then satisfied the curiosity of Eagles fans who wondered whether he could still throw by completing 20 of 30 passes for 247 yards and a touchdown in Philadelphia's 20-6 win. The Eagles were headed to the National Football Conference (NFC) championship game for the second year, and McNabb had led the way, less than two months after breaking his ankle.

It was yet another *virtuoso* performance by one of the NFL's top players. In just four years in the league, McNabb had become a star. More importantly, he was the Eagles' team leader and the man most responsible for pulling them out of the league's basement. "He's their Michael Jordan," New York Giants linebacker Micheal Barrow said. "Everything goes through him." Many would not have believed that possible only four years before. Had the Eagles not done so poorly back in 1998 (3-13), McNabb would never have become an Eagle. The awful finish allowed Philadelphia to pick second in the 1999 NFL Draft. The Eagles chose McNabb, even though many fans wanted the team to pick someone else. Four years later, even those grouches were convinced. McNabb was the Eagles' heart and soul.

"He can beat you with his hands, his head, his eyes, his feet, anything," said Tampa Bay Buccaneers defensive tackle Warren Sapp. "He's one of the best quarterbacks in the game, the ultimate weapon in the league."

McNabb has led the Eagles to the playoffs in each of his three years as a full-time starter and to the NFC title game twice. He has played in the Pro Bowl, the NFL's postseason all-star game, three times. He has also silenced critics who considered him to be little more than a running back with a big arm, as some had called African-American quarterbacks for years. He has also been one of the first successful African-American quarterbacks in the NFL. McNabb is a multitalented twenty-first century quarterback who combines great arm strength and tremendous speed with a quick mind and love of the game. Donovan specializes in delivering under pressure and loves to compete. "The

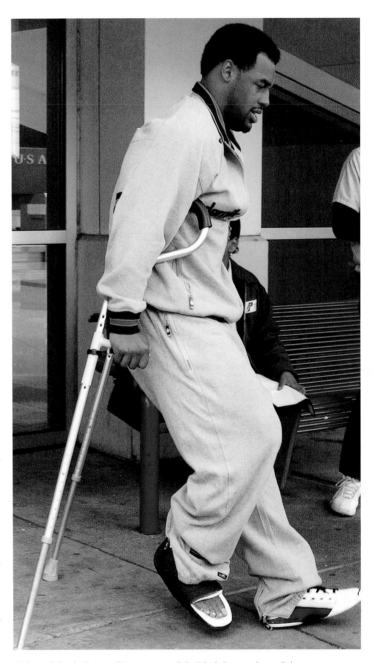

After his injury, Donovan McNabb makes his way through the airport on crutches instead of flying through the field.

Surrounded by family and friends, McNabb is all smiles after being chosen by the Philadelphia Eagles as the team's first draft pick in April 1999.

greater the challenge, the more he loves to attack it," Eagles head coach Andy Reid said. "The one overriding factor to all the questions is that he wants to be the best."

But McNabb is not just interested in successes on the field. He is involved in the community, has several *endorsement* deals, and even serves on the *board of trustees* at Syracuse University, from which he graduated with a degree in speech communications. Every year, he dresses up as Santa Claus and hands out toys to underprivileged children. He started a scholarship fund at Mt. Carmel High School in Chicago, from which he graduated. His parents, Wilma and Samuel, gave McNabb a strong sense of right and wrong. He lives by their teachings every day.

Many of the same great qualities that make McNabb so admired off the field combine to help him lead on it. His teammates do not just look to McNabb because he is the quarterback. He is a *classic* leader, not only capable of leading his troops into battle but also willing to stand beside them and fight. And when the work is done, McNabb is likely to sing a silly song or make people laugh with his dead-on impersonation of Reid.

"Donovan is not only a great football player, he's a great leader," Reid said. "That's very important, especially in the huddle, to get people to listen. With Donovan, it's like I have a coach out on the field [who] can take control. Not only that, he's . . .

unique, because he's respected by all positions.

"Sometimes, quarterbacks can *alienate* themselves from other members of the team. He doesn't do that. He makes his way around the locker room and gets everybody together."

Once the team is together, Donovan heads the charge into the fray. And success is usually the outcome.

Philadelphia Eagles coach Andy Reid gives McNabb some pointers during training camp in 2002.

Laughing on the stairs with family members, McNabb is at his most relaxed.

CHAPTER TWO

Laying the Foundation

The message was always the same. It did not matter whether the McNabb family was living in Chicago, where Donovan was born, or in the leafy suburb of Dolton, Illinois, where the family later moved. Samuel and Wilma McNabb preached the same thing, again and again. Be yourself. Don't try to please anybody else.

"That's something that's common sense, really," Donovan said. "When you get older, you can't worry about what people are saying about you. Once you do, then it takes away from what you are."

In November 1976, the country was just finishing the year-long celebration of its two-hundredth birthday. Meanwhile, the McNabbs were delighting in the birth of their second son, born four years after Sean. Donovan Jamal McNabb was born on November 25, 1976, in Chicago. Sam was an electrical engineer, and Wilma a registered nurse. They worked hard, and eventually they were able to give their two children the benefits of a stable home in Dolton. Donovan was eight when the family moved from Chicago's South Side, which was home to gangs, guns, and drugs.

Not that it was always easy. The McNabbs were one of the first African-American families to move to Dolton. Not long after they arrived, people who wished them no good broke into their house, knocked holes in the walls inside, and spray-painted obscenities on the outer walls. But the McNabbs were not about to leave. Sam and Wilma encouraged their children to be strong and brave. Soon, Donovan's outgoing personality won him plenty of friends in his new neighborhood. Later, when he was booed by Philadelphia fans on Draft Day, the message of his parents during those tough early years came back to him. "What we learned from our move to Dolton is that not everyone will be happy for you when you make a success of your life," Sam McNabb said.

> "**What we learned from our move to Dolton is that not everyone will be happy for you when you make a success of your life.**"
> —**Sam McNabb**

From the time he could walk, Donovan loved sports. He would tear pictures of athletes out of magazines and plaster them onto the walls of his room. But the person he admired most was Sean, who was a promising athlete. As a young boy, Donovan was the manager of one of the basketball teams for which Sean played. He still lists Sean as his idol,

McNabb's mother Wilma, always his greatest fan, looks on with delight as she learns that McNabb will become the highest-paid player in National Football League history.

Football Terms

Like all sports, football has its own language. Here are some popular terms and their definitions.

blitz—A defensive strategy in which a team sends extra players to rush the quarterback. A blitz tries to confuse the blockers by bringing rushers from many different parts of the field and also to outnumber the blockers. Quarterbacks must recognize when a blitz is coming and pass the ball quickly to avoid being tackled or sacked.

downfield—The parts of a field that are a long way off from the ball. When a quarterback throws the ball downfield, he is often passing deep to a receiver.

Heisman Trophy—The award given out each season to the best player in college football, as voted on by previous Heisman winners, sportswriters, broadcasters, former players, and coaches from around the country.

pocket—A safe area in which the quarterback can look for open receivers and make his throw. Offensive linemen create the pocket by working together to keep defenders away from the passer.

pursuit angle—The path a defender takes when he is trying to tackle the offensive player with the ball.

redshirts—College players who can practice with the team but are not allowed to play in games. That allows them to gain experience without using one of their four years of eligibility.

scrimmage—The imaginary line from which play begins. The offensive and defensive linemen take their stances along the line of scrimmage.

snap—The beginning of a play, when the center hands the ball through his legs to a quarterback. When the quarterback receives the ball, he has "taken the snap." Players who participate in many plays during a practice session are "taking a lot of snaps."

split-veer offense—An offense in which the quarterback is responsible for deciding on each play whether to hand the ball off to a running back, keep the ball himself and run, or pitch it to another running back. The quarterback has only a couple of seconds to make this decision.

third-stringer—A person who is listed third, behind the starter and backup, at a position on a football team. He would only play if the two men ahead of him were hurt or didn't perform well.

under center—The place from which a quarterback takes the snap to start a play. Because his hands are between the center's legs, he is considered "under" the center.

upfield—Heading in the direction of the goal line. When a player is heading upfield, he gains yards, often in large amounts.

even though Donovan is a professional quarterback, and Sean never advanced athletically beyond the high-school level. Sean stays close to his brother, helping him manage his day-to-day responsibilities.

"We used to think Donovan was going to grow up and be a comedian," Wilma said. "It looked like he was going to be another Eddie Murphy. But then he got serious about football."

That almost did not happen. At first, Wilma wouldn't let Donovan play. She feared he was too thin and would be injured too easily. She gave in only when the coach called and promised that Donovan would be safe. He was safe—and good. Donovan excelled on the gridiron and on the hoop court and loved to play both sports. "I mean he was *dominant* in grade school," said San Francisco 49ers wide receiver Tai Streets, who grew up in Donovan's neighborhood.

When it came time to choose a high school for Donovan, Sam and Wilma sent their son back to Mt. Carmel High School on the South Side of Chicago. The school was an oasis in a tough neighborhood. The 820-student, all-male Catholic school offered the type of *rigorous* academic curriculum that pleased Donovan's parents. Even though Donovan traveled more than an hour to and from school, the trip was worth it. At Mt. Carmel, he learned discipline and blended with a variety of students in an environment he would not have found in the suburbs.

"Mt. Carmel is in what might be described as a low-income area, but the school has always attracted good, very committed students from all over," said Dan O'Connor, a Mt. Carmel graduate and now a faculty member at the school. "I passed two other Catholic schools on my way here back then. I still do. But this is where I wanted to be. It's been that way for a lot of kids for a lot of years."

At Mt. Carmel, Donovan became a standout two-sport athlete. He played football with Simeon Rice, who is now a member of the Tampa Bay Buccaneers, the 2003 Super Bowl champs. He played basketball with Antoine Walker, an NBA All-Star with the Boston Celtics. On the basketball court, he helped Mt. Carmel to the Chicago Catholic League title during his senior

Philadelphia Eagles quarterback McNabb and Tampa Bay Buccaneers defensive end Simeon Rice have been friends since they played football together in high school. Now they are friendly rivals.

year. He averaged 17 points a game for a team which finished 25-4. He was even better on the football field.

Donovan was 23-3 as a starter at Mt. Carmel. He operated the team's split-veer offense, which relies heavily on the quarterback's ability to run and pass well, along with making quick decisions, like a magician. "Some of the stuff he would do in practice was so amazing

The first day of training camp for Philadelphia Eagles McNabb!

that it became normal seeing him do it in a game," said Mike Daigler, a backup quarterback at Mt. Carmel during Donovan's senior year. When Donovan's senior season ended, he was named to several high-school All-America teams and was sought after by many major-college football programs across the country. And for good reason. Donovan was a rare athlete, capable of dominating games by himself.

"We would have his receivers covered and every pursuit angle and running lane filled, have every part of the game defended, and McNabb would still make a big play out of nothing," said Todd Werner, then-coach of Mt. Carmel rival St. Rita High School. "He was so difficult to defend because of all the *intangibles* he brought to the game and because he has so much poise."

Chicago was impressed. It was time for Donovan to show the rest of the country what he could do.

Syracuse quarterback Donovan McNabb looks to pass during a game against Eastern Michigan on October 14, 1995.

CHAPTER THREE
College Days

It was a difficult decision. The kind you lose sleep over. The kind that chews you up inside.

It was the winter of 1998, and McNabb was faced with a tough reality. If he was going to be a great football player, the kind who makes NFL scouts drool, he had to get better. Much better. There was only one way to do that.

Quit basketball.

During his first two seasons at Syracuse University, McNabb had done what he wanted. He dazzled opponents on the football field and then hit the hardwood, where he played backup guard on the Orangemen's basketball team. The life he lived while at Mt. Carmel High School was a great life.

"Donovan used to be the court jester," Syracuse quarterback coach Kevin Rogers said. "He was happy-go-lucky, zip-a-dee-doo-dah, bumping bellies with offensive linemen. Now, he has work to do. Business is business."

Although McNabb saw limited action on the hoop court, he had been part of the Syracuse team that had reached the 1996 National Collegiate Athletic Association (NCAA) championship game before falling to Kentucky. As much fun as that had been, he

Donovan McNabb loves a good laugh. Here, the Syracuse quarterback clowns during the second half of a game against East Carolina on October 4, 1997. And Syracuse had the last laugh—the team won, 56-0.

had to admit his future was not as a basketball player. It was time to get serious. It was time to be a full-time football player.

"I think dedicating myself to football will be a bonus for the whole team," he said in the spring of 1998. "It lets my teammates know that [I am], and the other seniors are, extremely serious. This is my last year, so my focus lets them know how important it is for us to go out and make something happen this year."

It's not as if McNabb had been fooling around during his first three seasons as Syracuse's quarterback. He had been first string almost from the moment he arrived on campus in the late summer of 1994. McNabb sat out his first year as a redshirt. After that, he became Syracuse's full-time starter. He led the Orangemen to three bowl games in his first three years as a player. He was named Most Valuable Player (MVP) of the 1996 Gator Bowl for throwing three touchdown passes in a 41-0 *rout* of Clemson. But with just one year remaining at Syracuse, McNabb wanted to lead the Orangemen to a Big East Conference championship. He wanted to become the school's all-time leading passer. Even though he had thrown for 2,488 yards and 20 touchdowns in 1997, McNabb wanted more.

So, he went to work. During the off-season, McNabb improved his speed and strength. He embraced his role as a team leader. And it all paid off. The Orangemen began the 1998 campaign

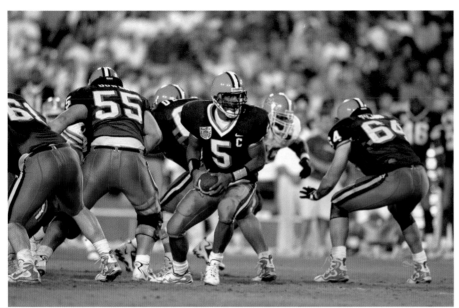

As usual, Syracuse quarterback McNabb is in the middle of the action—in this case, against Florida.

by losing a heartbreaking 34-33 decision to Tennessee, the team that would ultimately win the national title. But Syracuse then went to Michigan and, in front of more than 110,000 spectators, whipped the defending national champion Wolverines, 38-28. It became clear that McNabb was piloting one of the most powerful offenses in the nation. Syracuse pounded Rutgers, 70-14. It beat Cincinnati, 63-21. It scored more than 40 points against both Pittsburgh and Boston College. Then came the big challenges.

The first was in Syracuse's Carrier Dome home, against Virginia Tech. Things did not go well. The Hokies bolted to a 21-3 lead, and as the fourth quarter wound down, defeat seemed probable. The Orangemen trailed Tech, 26-21, with 4:42 remaining, and they had the ball on their own 17-yard line. Then McNabb took over. He led Syracuse down the field, running or passing on 12 of 14 plays. With 0:06 remaining, McNabb called a timeout, hobbled to the sideline on an ankle he had sprained earlier in the game, and promptly threw up because of fatigue. He summoned enough strength to throw a 13-yard touchdown pass to tight end Stephen Brominski as the clock reached 0:00. Syracuse had a 28-26 win, and McNabb had a performance for the ages. "He put the team on his back and said, 'Let's go,'" Rogers said.

After a win over Temple, McNabb led Syracuse against bitter rival Miami. The result was an improbable 66-13 pounding of the 22nd-ranked Hurricanes and the Big East title.

The NFL Draft

The first player ever drafted by the National Football League—University of Chicago's Jay Berwanger, back in 1936—didn't even sign with Philadelphia, the team that selected him. He thought he could make more money as a businessman than a football player. He was probably right.

That is not the case any more. Players selected by NFL teams are paid a lot of money, particularly those taken in the first round. And they certainly do not give up the chance to play professional football.

The draft, which takes place every April, allows NFL teams to add talent to their rosters by selecting players who have spent at least three years on a college campus. The draft consists of seven rounds, with each round made up of thirty-two selections. Teams are arranged in reverse order of their finish the previous season. For instance, the team with the worst record picks first in each round, while the Super Bowl champion chooses last.

Of course, not every round goes in that order. Throughout the year, teams make trades that often include future draft picks. A team might trade for another player and offer in return its fourth-round choice in the next draft. Each team prepares carefully for the draft, scouting as many players as possible, the better to make good use of its choices. A first-round choice is usually more highly regarded than a seventh-rounder, but there is no guarantee that either will become a star. The NFL is a much more difficult game than the college version, and some players can't make the jump successfully.

Although Syracuse ended its season by losing to Florida in the Orange Bowl, it had been a great year. McNabb was named the first-team All-Big East quarterback, the fourth time he had received that honor. He had set a Big East record for career touchdown passes with 77. And it became increasingly clear that he would be sought after by many NFL teams in the upcoming draft. Even though there were questions about the offense he ran at Syracuse, which involved more running by the quarterback than most NFL attacks, scouts were in agreement that McNabb had plenty of talent. "He gets the ball there," said one scout. "He makes good decisions. He moves around."

On Draft Day, Philadelphia picked McNabb second overall, behind University of

Kentucky quarterback Tim Couch, who went to the Cleveland Browns. Some of the Eagles fans who had made the trip up to New York for the draft booed the selection. They wanted Philadelphia to choose University of Texas running back Ricky Williams, who had won the Heisman Trophy as college football's best player.

> **"When I was booed, it definitely hurt, I look at it in a way as a motivating factor. I'm not worried about the boos."**
> **—Donovan McNabb**

"When I was booed, it definitely hurt," McNabb said. "I look at it in a way as a motivating factor. I'm not worried about the boos."

It wouldn't be long before McNabb turned those boos into cheers. Loud cheers.

Philadelphia Eagles'
Donovan McNabb is pulled
down by Washington Redskins'
Sam Shade. Although the
Eagles lost the play, they won
the game, 35-28.

CHAPTER FOUR
The Big Time

The moment finally came, on November 14, 1999. McNabb would be making his first NFL start, against the Washington Redskins. It was the dawn of a new era, the beginning of the Eagles' future. After more than five years of uncertainty at quarterback, the position was set. Or at least that's what everybody thought. McNabb was the Eagles' quarterback. Period.

"It's huge," then-center Steve Everitt said. "I think we're seeing the end of the revolving door. That should be pretty obvious. It's definitely important, not just for the other ten guys on offense, but for the quarterback. He doesn't have to look over his shoulder, and that's just huge."

McNabb had tried to be patient, but it wasn't easy. He was used to playing, not watching. But that's what he did for the first half of the season. Sure, he had played a series or two in most games, but the starting quarterback job had belonged to Doug Pederson, a good friend of Eagles coach Andy Reid. Pederson wasn't a star, but he was familiar with Reid's offensive system and would run the team until McNabb was ready. Then, Pederson would step aside. Of course, McNabb thought he was ready right away, especially when Cleveland's Tim Couch and Cincinnati's Akili Smith, also rookie quarterbacks, were playing full-time.

The Philadelphia Eagles and Their Fans

Eagles fans love their team—most of the time. They wear the team's colors proudly. They show up for games and make more noise than most NFL crowds. But Eagles fans are tough on everybody who plays in Philadelphia, whether they are visitors or members of the home team.

Philadelphia fans consider it their right to boo athletes. If an Eagles player is not performing the way they think he should, they will let him know it, loudly. Even if they cheered him just a moment ago, the fans are likely to boo if he makes a mistake.

In 1999, a local sports talk radio host rented a bus and brought thirty fans—he called them "The Dirty Thirty"—to New York for the NFL draft. The host believed the Eagles should draft Ricky Williams, a running back from the University of Texas who had won the Heisman Trophy. He even enlisted the help of Philadelphia mayor Ed Rendell in his cause.

Rendell called Eagles coach Andy Reid and asked him to pick Williams. But Reid and the Eagles chose Donovan McNabb. "The Dirty Thirty" booed. Rendell criticized the pick. When Donovan arrived in Philadelphia, though, he gave the mayor an Eagles jersey bearing Williams's number 34 in the front and his own 5 in the back. Everybody cheered. They haven't stopped since.

"They're getting experience firsthand," McNabb said. "To see that and not be a part of that, it hits you a little bit hard. They're in different situations, I guess. All I can do is see what's happening here in my season."

McNabb had arrived late for his first training camp, after contract negotiations had dragged out. He finally signed a seven-year, $54 million deal that included a bonus of $11 million just for signing the contract. The deal made him the highest-paid player in Eagles history. And he wanted to earn it right away. But the job was Pederson's, and McNabb had to wait. When he did get to play, it was obvious he had much to learn. In the Eagles' ugly Week 2, 19-5 loss to Tampa Bay, McNabb completed 4 of 11 passes for 26 yards. It wasn't exactly a dreamy debut.

"I'm not excited about my performance at all," McNabb said after the game. "I don't think I played well."

That's how it went the first half of the season. McNabb struggled, although he did show occasional flashes. He completed 6 of 11 passes for 34 yards in a loss to Buffalo. And on November 7, he was 8 of 20 for 68 yards versus Carolina. That was the day Reid decided McNabb would be his starter. For good. So, when the Eagles took the field against the Redskins, McNabb was under center. Though his numbers weren't great (8 of 21, 60 yards), he led the Eagles to a 35-28 win. A new era had dawned. The Eagles finished the season 5-11, but McNabb made big strides by season's end. He even led Philly to a win over powerful St. Louis in the season's final game. Things weren't perfect, but the future looked bright.

"I'm learning about the game," McNabb said late in the season. "How long 'til I get it? I can't say when. But I have confidence. It's just so hard on a quarterback. One game you throw for 300 yards, then against a team that game-plans you different, you only throw for 150."

The Eagles players, coaches, and fans entered the 2000 season with

Eagles quarterback McNabb pushes away Arizona Cardinals' Pat Tillman as he rushes for a touchdown in the third quarter of a game on November 19, 2000. The Eagles won, 34-9.

tremendous optimism. The young team was growing together, and pieces were being put into place. The biggest was at quarterback, and McNabb was ready to go. Even though he had to spend part of the off-season working to rehabilitate an injured knee, McNabb came to camp in great shape, stronger, faster, and more experienced than he had been his rookie season.

"He's so much better than he was last year," Eagles defensive coordinator Jimmy Johnson said. "He's way ahead, just in picking up blitzes. He's a guy who can scramble. He's a solid quarterback, and he's only going to keep getting better."

Johnson was right. McNabb was ready to make a jump. And what a jump it was. By the time 2000 was over, McNabb had accounted for almost 75 percent of the team's total offense, thanks to his big arm and strong legs. He threw for 3,365 yards and 21 touchdowns. He ran for 629 more and scored six times. During one November stretch, McNabb led the Eagles to four straight wins, two of which came in overtime. In the December 10 game at Cleveland, he threw for 390 yards and four touchdowns. It was an amazing performance. McNabb was so good that he finished second in the balloting for the NFL's Most Valuable Player, to St. Louis running back Marshall Faulk. The Eagles went 11-5 and dumped Tampa Bay in the first round of the playoffs.

> "They're getting experience firsthand. To see that and not be a part of that, it hits you a little bit hard. They're in different situations, I guess. All I can do is see what's happening here in my season."
>
> —Donovan McNabb

"For the last five years, we've been shuffling around at quarterback," Eagles cornerback Troy Vincent said. "I think that was our biggest problem, just trying to find out who's going to be the heart and soul of this football team. Teams don't win without the QB. We have that now."

More importantly, McNabb won over the team. He was great on the field. Off it, he was a leader, reaching out to players on offense and defense. He kept making people laugh and was even caught by Reid once for imitating the coach.

McNabb reached out to the community more. And the fans reached back. Many apologized to him for the booing that accompanied the announcement of his selection on

Philadelphia Eagles' McNabb jumps over teammate Jermane Mayberry and Redskins' Mark Carrier in the first quarter of a game.

Draft Day. The Eagles were Donovan's team, and that meant good things for the future.

"If I look out on that field during a fourth-and-one situation late in the game and see him cracking a smile, I'll have no doubt we're in control," said safety Damon Moore.

The Eagles and Donovan were in control. And things were only going to get better.

Philadelphia Eagles quarterback Donovan McNabb fumbles as the New York Giants go on to a 20-10 victory on January 7, 2001.

CHAPTER FIVE

On the Verge

McNabb had finished second in the MVP voting his second year in the league. He had led the Eagles to a playoff win. He had dazzled fans and opponents with his many talents. But this was bigger. This was Monday Night Football. This was against the New York Giants, the Eagles' chief rivals. This was the team that had knocked Philly out of the playoffs the season before.

And McNabb was laying an egg. The Eagles' offense couldn't do anything in the first half against the Giants. It couldn't get it going in the third quarter, either. New York led, 9-3, late in the fourth quarter, and the Eagles were in trouble. It was just like the playoff game, which the Giants won, 20-10. McNabb couldn't put it together then, either. But that didn't mean McNabb had quit.

"He didn't hang his head," Eagles coach Andy Reid said. "He kept firing, and you have to do that at his position. You can't have any hesitation, and Donovan didn't."

With it all on the line, late in the game, McNabb took over. He led the Eagles on a drive downfield, mixing his runs and throws perfectly. When he connected on a touchdown pass with James Thrash, the Eagles had a 10-9 win in front of a delirious home crowd and a *Monday Night Football* audience. "There are some things, as a young quarterback, that you have to do if you are going to be one of the top quarterbacks in the NFL," Reid said.

African-American Quarterbacks

For many years, African Americans did not play quarterback in the NFL. Some coaches thought they were too fast to use there and used them as running backs, receivers, or defensive backs. Others didn't think they were smart enough, a theory that has been proven wrong many times.

African Americans started to play that position in the 1970s. At that time, James Harris started for the Los Angeles Rams and San Diego Chargers. And Doug Williams played for the Tampa Bay Buccaneers in the 1970s and early 1980s. He led the Washington Redskins to the Super Bowl title, in 1988.

In the 1990s, more and more African Americans started to excel as NFL quarterbacks. Part of the reason was that high school and college teams made more use of them at the position, preparing them to play quarterback professionally. Once there, they began to experience great success. Today, the NFL has plenty of African-American stars at quarterback, including Philadelphia's Donovan McNabb, Minnesota's Daunte Culpepper, Atlanta's Michael Vick, Tennessee's Steve McNair, and New Orleans's Aaron Brooks.

It was a huge win for the Eagles, who had started the season 2-2. And it was another example of how McNabb was growing into one of the NFL's best. After the game, ESPN-TV reporter Chris Mortensen likened McNabb to basketball great Michael Jordan, who was known for his late-game heroics. McNabb was similar to Jordan in another way: like Jordan, McNabb always worked hard during the off-season. McNabb arrived at training camp in 2001 after spending his off-season laboring in the Phoenix heat, which sometimes reached 115 degrees Fahrenheit (46° Celsius). He had moved there for part of the winter so that he could test himself in the harsh climate. He lifted weights. Ran extra sprints. Improved his balance. He even did special eye exercises to improve his *peripheral vision.* He threw hundreds of passes. He became more mentally tough through forcing himself to work when his mind and body were tired. "Donovan's a happy, caring, loving guy most of the time," said Tim McClellan, who oversees McNabb's off-season workouts. "But when something has to get done, it gets done."

The Eagles entered 2001 hoping to win their division, the NFC East, and make a run at the Super Bowl. Those were big goals, but with McNabb at quarterback, anything was possible. Though the Eagles beat the Giants to move to 3-2, they had some moments of doubt throughout the rest of the season. At one point, they were 6-4. After a December loss to San Francisco, the Philadelphia media began to criticize McNabb. They cited his relatively low completion percentage (58.1 percent) and his struggle against the better teams on the Eagles' schedule. With a rematch looming against the Giants for the NFC East title, McNabb needed to improve.

And that's what he did. In perhaps the most impressive performance of his young career, McNabb led the Eagles to a thrilling 24-21 victory. Whenever the Eagles needed a big play, he delivered. When Philly was

Philadelphia Eagles' Donovan McNabb relishes his touchdown against the Seattle Seahawks on September 23, 2001. The Eagles won, 27-3.

down, 10-7, in the fourth quarter, he threw a 57-yard touchdown pass to James Thrash, making it 14-10, Eagles. But the Giants rallied and took a 21-14 lead, with 2:33 to play. So, McNabb went to work again. He led the Eagles on a 67-yard drive and threw a 7-yard touchdown pass to tight end Chad Lewis with 1:49 to go, tying the score at 21. Then, with less than a minute left, McNabb drove the Eagles 54 yards to set up David Akers's game-winning 35-yard field goal, with 0:07 remaining. The Eagles had the win and the division title.

Philadelphia Eagles quarterback Donovan McNabb is chased by the Chicago Bears during the fourth quarter of the National Football Conference Divisional playoff in Chicago on January 19, 2002. The Eagles defeated the Bears, 33-19.

"Donovan stepped up and did a [great] job under about as much pressure as you are going to have," Reid said. "He hung right in there and took control of the huddle."

The postseason featured more success and more McNabb. He led the Eagles to an easy 31-9 rout of Tampa Bay in the first round of the playoffs. That earned the Eagles a chance to play the Bears in Chicago, McNabb's hometown. It was quite a homecoming. A few days before the game, Wilma McNabb catered a banquet for the Eagles featuring all of Donovan's favorites—turkey, macaroni and cheese, red beans and rice, and peach cobbler. Then, McNabb and the Eagles feasted on the Bears in a 33-19 win. He completed 26 of 40 passes for 262 yards and two scores. He also ran for 37 yards.

"He beat us," Bears defensive tackle Keith Traylor said. "He beat us running. He beat us throwing. A [few] times, I did see where he was running and he ended up throwing the ball to a guy who was wide open. I don't know what happened, but he was very successful."

"Donovan stepped up and did a [great] job under about as much pressure as you are going to have. He hung right in there and took control of the huddle."
—Andy Reid

McNabb enjoyed the whole week, but he knew he was in Chicago on business, rather than to have fun. "I had a great time seeing all my family and friends and eating all my mom's food," he said. "But today I knew what I had to do."

Only one team stood between the Eagles and the Super Bowl, the St. Louis Rams. It would be an epic battle. And with time running out in the fourth quarter and the Eagles trailing, 29-24, McNabb had one last chance at some magic. The Eagles reached their own 48 but ran out of downs. There would be no miracle comeback, no Super Bowl. But it had been a great year.

There was no denying that. McNabb and the Eagles would be back.

"I learned [this year] that you have to stay aggressive," McNabb said. "You have to take chances. Sometimes, your chances might end up going the other way."

Most of the time, though, they work out. McNabb proved that in 2001.

Philadelphia Eagles' Donovan McNabb celebrates the Eagles' win against the Chicago Bears in the playoffs.

After sitting out most of the 2002 season with an ankle injury, Philadelphia Eagles' McNabb answers questions at a January 2003 press conference.

CHAPTER SIX

The Promised Land—Almost

It looked like a completely ordinary play. McNabb was under pressure in the pocket and trying to make something happen. He had done it hundreds of times during his career. A step here. A quick move. A dip of the hip. Freedom.

Not this time. Arizona Cardinals defenders Adrian Wilson and LeVar Woods corralled McNabb and sent him crashing to the turf. As he landed, McNabb's right ankle bent horribly to one side. Television replays showed that this wasn't just a slight roll. This one was bad.

McNabb lay on the cold, wet Veterans Stadium turf as Eagles fans everywhere tried to remain calm. It was just the third play of the game, and he was hurt. McNabb rose to his feet and hobbled off the field, grimacing, to a somewhat restrained ovation. His ankle was throbbing. But McNabb wasn't looking for the doctor. "I just blocked the pain out," he said.

McNabb returned to the game and limped through a magnificent performance that may have been the bravest show Eagles fans had ever seen. He completed 20 of 25 passes for 255 yards and 4 touchdowns in a 38-14 win, with a broken ankle. Postgame *X-rays* revealed that McNabb had a fractured fibula, the major bone in the lower part of the leg. He would need six to eight weeks of rest and rehabilitation.

Donovan McNabb, starting quarterback for the Philadelphia Eagles, goes down with a snap of his ankle during a game against the Arizona Cardinals on November 17, 2002.

"It's a surprise to hear how bad he's hurt," Eagles linebacker Ike Reese said. "But it's even more of a surprise that he was able to stay in and play the whole game."

McNabb wouldn't be playing for a while, not after breaking his ankle. And that would be hard to do. He started 45 of 48 possible games while at Syracuse. He never missed a contest in high school. And since taking over the starting reins with Philadelphia during his rookie year, he missed just one start, against New England in 1999, when he hurt his knee. Inactivity was not the best thing for Donovan McNabb. "I just want to accept the fact that I'm a little banged up," he said after the game.

The Eagles had to accept it, too. Their leader, the man who had led them to a 7-3 record and first place in the NFC East, was done for the rest of the regular season and perhaps for the playoffs. The team's Super Bowl dreams were in jeopardy. The season was in trouble. "Anytime your prime-time player goes down, other players have to step up," Eagles running back Duce Staley said.

McNabb had been excellent to date. He was most impressive in a 17-3 Monday night

> **"It's a surprise to hear how bad he's hurt. But it's even more of a surprise that he was able to stay in and play the whole game."**
> **—Ike Reese**

Donovan McNabb loves to kid around—and to make kids happy. He signs autographs for sick children at Ronald McDonald House while recovering from a broken ankle.

victory over the Giants. In that game, he rushed for 111 yards, more yards than all the New York backs had gained. One week earlier, he had led the Eagles to an important, 20-10 win over Tampa Bay and its excellent defense. Things looked good. A playoff berth was almost a certainty. Then came the injury.

The Eagles didn't quit. In fact, they won five of their next six games, behind backup quarterbacks Koy Detmer and A. J. Feeley. Philadelphia was the NFC East Division champion again. And the team's 12-4 record assured it of home-field advantage in the playoffs. If the Eagles were playing a postseason game other than the Super Bowl, which would be played in San Diego, it would be at Veterans Stadium. And while the Eagles took care of that business, McNabb tended to his rehabilitation. His *cardiovascular* workouts were so tough that the trainers had to work with him in shifts. He was tiring them out! He hit the weights. He worked in the pool. As time moved on, McNabb took snaps from center, dropped back, and threw. He felt good and determined to be ready for the playoffs.

"I'll be ready," he said as the post-season

McNabb is all smiles as he heads for training camp after his broken ankle has healed.

approached. "It's going to be exciting, and I'm going to have a lot of fun with it."

The players responded, too. When McNabb stepped under center in a live practice drill, there was excitement and enthusiasm. "It was a spark for us," receiver Todd Pinkston said. "Just having him out there was great. His drive and his leadership are important for everyone."

So, McNabb led. He guided the Eagles to a 20-6 win over the upstart Falcons in the post-season's second round, clinching the victory with a fourth-down touchdown pass to James Thrash. The win earned the Eagles a rematch with Tampa Bay, the team Philadelphia had beaten during the regular season and in the playoffs two years running. It would be a battle for the Super Bowl, and the Eagles felt confident. They had the home crowd. They were playing the last football game at the Vet. (The Eagles moved into a new home for the 2003 season.) It would be a cold day, something their Florida guests wouldn't enjoy. And they had McNabb.

Early on, it looked like an Eagles rout. Duce Staley scored on a 20-yard run on the game's second play, giving the Birds a 7-0 advantage. But Tampa Bay fought back to take a 10-7 lead. The Eagles tied it early in the second half, but that was it for Philadelphia's scoring. Tampa Bay took control and won, 27-10. It wasn't a good day for McNabb, who lost two fumbles, threw an interception that was returned for a touchdown, and didn't look sharp. Maybe he wasn't completely recovered from his injury, after all. For the second straight year, the Eagles had come up one game short in their drive to the Super Bowl.

"I played poorly," Donovan admitted after the game. "I'm being a man about it. We have enough players on this team. We just didn't play well at all."

It was a rare misstep at a crucial time for McNabb. But he was able to take heart at having helped the Eagles to the NFC title game two years in a row. There would be other chances to win. And odds were that he would.

Indeed, the 2003 season dawned with great promise for McNabb and the Eagles. Two straight trips to the NFC title game had established them as serious Super Bowl contenders. And the team's fans wanted nothing less than a trip to the Big Game. But trouble came quickly. The Eagles slumped to a 0-2 start, losing their first game in brand-new Lincoln Financial Field to Tampa Bay and then dropping a decision to New England.

> "I'll be ready. It's going to be exciting, and I'm going to have a lot of fun with it."
> —Donovan McNabb

McNabb didn't play well in either game, completing only 45 of his passes for 334 yards, three interceptions, and no touchdowns. While Eagles fans and local media wondered what was wrong, Rush Limbaugh, a radio talk-show host who was providing analysis for ESPN's pre-game show, said that the media and league were rooting for McNabb to be successful because he was an African American. The statement led to Limbaugh's resignation from the network and forced McNabb to take time away from game preparation to address the issue. He did so with dignity, but the whole situation made what had begun difficult even tougher. But no one was really worried.

McNabb had already proven himself a world-class player, and it was clear he would have a chance to prove that again and again.

Stats *Donovan McNabb*

Born: November 25, 1976
Birthplace: Chicago, Illinois
Height: 6' 2" (188 cm)
Weight: 240 pounds (109 kg)
College: Syracuse University
Team   Philadelphia Eagles
Position: Quarterback

Season	Team	Games	S	Att	Cmp	Cmp%	Yds	TDs	Int	Rush Yds	Rush TDs
1999	Eagles	12	6	216	106	49.1	948	8	7	313	0
2000	Eagles	16	16	569	330	58.0	3365	21	13	629	6
2001	Eagles	16	16	493	285	57.8	3233	25	12	482	2
2002	Eagles	10	10	361	211	58.4	2289	17	6	460	6

S = Games started, Att = Attempted passes, Cmp = Pass completions, Cmp% = Pass completion percentage, Yds = Yards gained passing, TDs = Touchdown passes, Int = Intercepted passes, Rush Yds = Yards gained rushing, Rush TDs = Touchdown rushes (runs)

Figures compiled from www.nfl.com

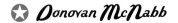

GLOSSARY

alienate—To cause people to dislike you by your actions or words.

board of trustees—A group of important people who help make the rules and decisions at a college or university.

cardiovascular—Of, or related to, the system of the body that includes the heart and the veins and arteries, which carry the blood. Athletes want to make their cardiovascular systems stronger, so they will be able to run and compete at high levels over longer periods of time.

classic—Being good enough to be remembered for many years. A classic game or performance is one that will be spoken of and written about for a long time.

dominant—Being so strong and talented that one is much better than everyone else.

endorsement—A sign of approval by a person or organization. A coach can endorse a player by telling the team or the media that the player is talented. Someone can endorse a product by participating in advertising that makes the product seem appealing.

intangibles—Qualities in a person that are hard to define but help that person become successful. A great athlete will often have a set of intangible abilities that add to his obvious skills.

peripheral vision—Being at the farthest boundaries of something. A person's peripheral vision includes the farthest things he can see when he looks up, down, or to the side.

rigorous—Extremely difficult. A set of tasks that forces a person to work quite hard and build strength over time.

rout—A win over an opponent by a large amount of points.

virtuoso—A performance of great skill and style. Someone who is capable of achieving excellence often.

X-ray—A way to examine people by photographing their insides.

FIND OUT MORE

Books

Steenkamer, Paul. *Sports Greats: Donovan McNabb*. Berkeley Heights, NJ: Enslow Publishers, Inc., 2003.

Web Sites

Official NFL Site
http://www.NFL.com/players/playerpage/13361

Sports Illustrated/CNN Site
http://www.sportsillustrated.cnn.com/football/nfl/players/4650/

INDEX

Page numbers in **boldface** are illustrations.

All-America high-school teams, 18
All-Big East quarterback, first-team, 24

basketball, playing of, 14, 16–17, 21–22
blitz, 15, 30
board of trustees, 10

cardiovascular, 41, 46
classic, 10, 46
community service, 10, **41**
contract negotiations, 14, 28
Couch, Tim, 25, 27

"Dirty Thirty, The," 28
Dolton, Illinois, residence in, 13, 14
dominant, 16
downfield, 15, 23
Draft Day, 9, **10**, 14, 24, 25, 28, 30

endorsement, 10

fans, 28, 29, 30, 39, 43
Feeley, A. J., 7, 41
football terms, 15

Heisman Trophy, 15, 25, 28

injuries, 7, 8, **8**, **9**, 23, 29, **38**, 39–40, **40**, 41, **41**, 42–43, **42**
intangibles, 19

leadership quality, 10, 11, 17–18, 22–23, 25, 30, 33, 36, 42
Limbaugh, Rush, 43

McNabb, Samuel, 10, **12**, 13, 16
McNabb, Sean, **12**, 13, 16
McNabb, Wilma, **10**, **12**, 13, **14**, 16, 36
Most Valuable Player (MVP), 22, 30, 33
Mt. Carmel High School, 10, 16–17, 18, 19, 21, 40

National Collegiate Athletic Association (NCAA), 21–22
National Football Conference (NFC) East championship, 8, 22, 24, 34, 35, 40, 41, 43

New York Giants, 8, **32**, 33, 35

Orangemen's basketball team, 21, 22, 23, **22**, **23**

parents, 10, **10**, **12**, 13, 14, 16, 36
passing, **6**, 8, **20**, 22, 23, 24, 28, 33, 34, 35, 43
Pederson, Doug, 27, 28
peripheral vision, 34, 56
Philadelphia Eagles, **6**, 7–11, **11**, 14, **17**, **18**, 24, 25, **26**, 27–31, **31**, **32**, 33–37, **36**, **37**, **38**, 40–43, **40**
playoffs, 7, 9, 30, 33, 36, **36**, **37**, 40, 41, 42

quarterbacks, 9, 10, 11, 15, 16, **17**, 18, **20**, 22, **22**, **23**, 27, 29, **29**, 30, **32**, 33, **36**
   African-American, 9, 34, 43

redshirts, 15, 22
Reid, Andy, 7, 10, 11, **11**, 27, 28, 30, 33, 36
Rice, Simeon, 16, **17**
rigorous, 16, 46
Rogers, Kevin, 21, 23
rout, 22

scrimmage, 7, 15
snap, 15
   from center, 41
   taking the, 15
split-veer offense, 15, 17
Staley, Duce, 40, 42
starting, 9, 15, 22, 28, 40
statistics, 22, 28, 29, 35, 36, 39, 41, 43, 45
Super Bowl, 16, 24, 34, 37, 40, 41, 43
Syracuse University, 10, **20**, 21, 22, 23, 24, 40

Tampa Bay Buccaneers, 9, 16, **17**, 28, 30, 34, 36, 41, 42, 43
Thrash, James, 33, 35, 42
touchdowns, 8, **29**, 30, 33, 35, 42
training camp, **11**, **18**, 34, **42**

Veterans Stadium, 39, 41, 42
virtuoso, 8, 46

Washington Redskins, **26**, 27, 29, **31**, 34
Web sites, 47
Williams, Ricky, 25, 28

X-ray, 39